AWARENESS
SCIENCE

Book - 2

Internet linked
(Linked Internet Sites given with topics to open out the world to the child)

MUKUL SAHGAL

S. CHAND & COMPANY LTD.

(AN ISO 9001 : 2000 COMPANY)
RAM NAGAR, NEW DELHI - 110055

S. CHAND & COMPANY LTD.
(An ISO 9001 : 2000 Company)

Head Office: 7361, RAM NAGAR, NEW DELHI - 110 055
Phone: 23672080-81-82, 9899107446, 9911310888
Fax: 91-11-23677446
Shop at: **schandgroup.com;** *e-mail:* **info@schandgroup.com**

Branches :

AHMEDABAD : 1st Floor, Heritage, Near Gujarat Vidhyapeeth, Ashram Road, **Ahmedabad** - 380 014, Ph: 27541965, 27542369, ahmedabad@schandgroup.com

BENGALURU : No. 6, Ahuja Chambers, 1st Cross, Kumara Krupa Road, **Bengaluru** - 560 001, Ph: 22268048, 22354008, bangalore@schandgroup.com

BHOPAL : Bajaj Tower, Plot No. 243, Lala Lajpat Rai Colony, Raisen Road, **Bhopal** - 462 011, Ph: 4274723. bhopal@schandgroup.com

CHANDIGARH : S.C.O. 2419-20, First Floor, Sector - 22-C (Near Aroma Hotel), **Chandigarh** -160 022, Ph: 2725443, 2725446, chandigarh@schandgroup.com

CHENNAI : 152, Anna Salai, **Chennai** - 600 002, Ph: 28460026, 28460027, chennai@schandgroup.com

COIMBATORE : No. 5, 30 Feet Road, Krishnasamy Nagar, Ramanathapuram, **Coimbatore** -641045, Ph: 0422-2323620 coimbatore@schandgroup.com **(Marketing Office)**

CUTTACK : 1st Floor, Bhartia Tower, Badambadi, **Cuttack** - 753 009, Ph: 2332580; 2332581, cuttack@schandgroup.com

DEHRADUN : 1st Floor, 20, New Road, Near Dwarka Store, **Dehradun** - 248 001, Ph: 2711101, 2710861, dehradun@schandgroup.com

GUWAHATI : Pan Bazar, **Guwahati** - 781 001, Ph: 2738811, 2735640 guwahati@schandgroup.com

HYDERABAD : Padma Plaza, H.No. 3-4-630, Opp. Ratna College, Narayanaguda, **Hyderabad** - 500 029, Ph: 24651135, 24744815, hyderabad@schandgroup.com

JAIPUR : A-14, Janta Store Shopping Complex, University Marg, Bapu Nagar, **Jaipur** - 302 015, Ph: 2719126, jaipur@schandgroup.com

JALANDHAR : Mai Hiran Gate, **Jalandhar** - 144 008, Ph: 2401630, 5000630, jalandhar@schandgroup.com

JAMMU : 67/B, B-Block, Gandhi Nagar, **Jammu** - 180 004, (M) 09878651464 **(Marketing Office)**

KOCHI : Kachapilly Square, Mullassery Canal Road, Ernakulam, **Kochi** - 682 011, Ph: 2378207, cochin@schandgroup.com

KOLKATA : 285/J, Bipin Bihari Ganguli Street, **Kolkata** - 700 012, Ph: 22367459, 22373914, kolkata@schandgroup.com

LUCKNOW : Mahabeer Market, 25 Gwynne Road, Aminabad, **Lucknow** - 226 018, Ph: 2626801, 2284815, lucknow@schandgroup.com

MUMBAI : Blackie House, 103/5, Walchand Hirachand Marg, Opp. G.P.O. **Mumbai** - 400 001, Ph: 22690881, 22610885, mumbai@schandgroup.com

NAGPUR : Karnal Bag, Model Mill Chowk, Umrer Road, **Nagpur** - 440 032, Ph: 2723901, 2777666 nagpur@schandgroup.com

PATNA : 104, Citicentre Ashok, Govind Mitra Road, **Patna** - 800 004, Ph: 2300489, 2302100, patna@schandgroup.com

PUNE : 291/1, Ganesh Gayatri Complex, 1st Floor, Somwarpeth, Near Jain Mandir, **Pune** - 411 011, Ph: 64017298, pune@schandgroup.com **(Marketing Office)**

RAIPUR : Kailash Residency, Plot No. 4B, Bottle House Road, Shankar Nagar, **Raipur** - 492 007, Ph: 09981200834, raipur@schandgroup.com **(Marketing Office)**

RANCHI : Flat No. 104, Sri Draupadi Smriti Apartments, East of Jaipal Singh Stadium, Neel Ratan Street, Upper Bazar, **Ranchi** - 834 001, Ph: 2208761, ranchi@schandgroup.com **(Marketing Office)**

SILIGURI : 122, Raja Ram Mohan Roy Road, East Vivekanandapally, P.O., **Siliguri**-734001, Dist., Jalpaiguri, (W.B.) Ph. 0353-2520750 **(Marketing Office)**

VISAKHAPATNAM: Plot No. 7, 1st Floor, Allipuram Extension, Opp. Radhakrishna Towers, Seethammadhara North Extn., **Visakhapatnam** - 530 013, (M) 09347580841, visakhapatnam@schandgroup.com **(Marketing Office)**

First Edition 1998
Subsequent Editions and Reprints 1999, 2001 (Twice), 2002, 2003, 2004, 2005, 2006, 2007, 2008, 2009, 2010 (Twice)
Reprint 2011

ISBN : 81-219-2669-6   **Code : 05 102**

PRINTED IN INDIA

By Rajendra Ravindra Printers Pvt. Ltd., 7361, Ram Nagar, New Delhi -110 055 and published by S. Chand & Company Ltd., 7361, Ram Nagar, New Delhi -110 055.

To Teachers and Parents

The teaching of science should be aimed at developing a scientific attitude in children rather than simply providing information. To achieve this, teachers must emphasize understanding of concepts, development of independent thinking and experimental skills, arousing curiosity to know more so that the child is not enclosed in a shell defined by the syllabus, and development of ability to apply knowledge in everyday situations.

This revised edition of Awareness Science takes special care to include features that assist teachers in meeting these objectives.

- NEW ◆ Carefully selected **full colour photographs** have been used to create interest by giving children a taste of the 'real thing'.
- ◆ **Concept learning** is encouraged by laying emphasis on understanding rather than merely providing information. The 'known to unknown' and 'simple to complex' approaches have been followed.
- NEW ◆ **Warming up!** makes the children think and participate, and thus improves motivation to learn.
- ◆ The '**Discuss in class and answer**' questions encourage independent thinking and applications of the principles learnt, through discussion and presentation of ideas.
- ◆ The '**Project**' in each chapter lays emphasis on 'learning by doing'.
- ◆ The '**Awareness beyond the classroom**' section* widens the horizon of the child, and arouses curiosity to know more.
- NEW ◆ Finally the **site addresses** provided in each chapter open out the world to the child through the Internet** – the child can learn more about whatever arouses his curiosity, as his own pace. This develops the much needed research skills.

Author

---

* We recommend that children study this section on their own, followed by discussions in class. The children should not be tested on this section.

** Teacher/Parent assistance is necessary until the child learns to use the Internet on his/her own.

Contents

1. Types of Plants

Warming Up!

You can see different sizes of plants around you. Do you think all of them will grow up to be tall and strong trees?

You can see different types of plants in a park or a garden. Some plants are tall and strong. Some are small.

• Trees

Tall and strong plants are **trees**.
They have a thick brown stem called a **trunk**.
They have many branches. Trees have different shapes. They live for many years.
A banyan tree can live for hundreds of years.

fir

banyan

banana

mango

To the Teacher

While repeating much of what we did in Book 1, we introduce a few more details. The children should be motivated to observe plants more closely. The concept of classification according to properties such as size, where they grow, etc., should be given due importance. Encourage the children to come up with their own criteria for classification, for the concept of classification is very important and is universally used in all branches of science. Let children realize that some plants will grow up to be trees but others will remain small.

coconut

neem

Large number of trees grow together in a **forest**.

a forest

LINKED INTERNET SITES

Learn about trees. http://www.urbanext.uiuc.edu/trees1/index.html
and http://www.urbanext.uiuc.edu/trees2/index.html

• Shrubs

Shrubs are smaller than trees.
They have hard and thin stems.
They have many branches.
They live for several years.

rose

bougainvillea

cotton

• Herbs

Herbs are small plants.
They have soft green stems.
Most common herbs live only for a few months.

rice

tomato

coriander

mint

• Climbers

Some plants have weak stems. They cannot stand straight.
They either grow along the ground, or grow up using a support.
They are **climbers**.

Many climbers such as pea and bean live for a few months only.
But others such as money plant and grape vine live for a few years.

bean

pea

grape vine

money plant

Remember

1. There are many kinds of plants.
2. Trees are tall and strong plants.
3. Shrubs are smaller than trees. They have hard stems.
4. Herbs are small plants with soft green stems.
5. Climbers have weak stems. They need support to climb up.

Exercises

1. Name the plants and say whether these are trees, shrubs, herbs or climbers? Write in the space provided.

Name ....

Type ....

Name ....

Type ....

2. Give the names of three plants that live for a few months only.

....

3. Give the names of three plants that live for several years.

....

4. What are these called?

(a) Very small plants. ....

(b) Plants with weak stems. ....

(c) Plants with soft green stems. ....

(d) Plants with thick brown stems. ....

Project

Make a plant scrap book

Collect pictures of plants. Paste them in a scrap book. Give two pages to each plant. Below each, draw a picture of its leaf and flower.

On the opposite page write what type of plant it is.

Leave some space blank on each page.

As you learn more about plants, we will ask you to write more things about them and draw more pictures in the blank space.

2. Where Plants Grow

Warming Up!

Collect pictures of different types of places such as hills, seashore, desert and plains. Observe the plants growing in these places. Can you see any difference in the types of plants?

Plants grow everywhere. Most plants grow on land.

fir

mango

neem

Some plants grow in cold places.

Some plants grow in warm places.

coconut

cactus

Some plants grow in hot places near the sea.

Some plants grow in deserts where there is very little water.

To the Teacher

The objective here is only to make the children aware that different plants grow in places with different climates. Only a few common climatic areas have been taken up. Our aim is not to provide complete information, which will come in later classes.

waterlily

Some plants grow in water.

tapegrass

Some plants grow underwater also.

Remember

1. Plants grow on land, in water, and even underwater.
2. Different kinds of plants grow in different places.

LINKED INTERNET SITES

Learn all about plants by solving cases!
http://www.urbanext.uiuc.edu/gpe/gpe.html

Exercises

1. Name one plant each that grows in these places:

(a) Cold places ....

(b) Warm places ....

(c) Hot places near the sea ....

(d) In water ....

(e) Underwater ....

Project

Where they grow

In your scarp book,
write where each plant normally grows.

3. Food from Plants

Warming Up!

Food is cooked in your kitchen. You eat this food to get energy and to grow. Left over food is stored in the refrigerator. What about plants? Do they need food? Where do they get food from? What do they do with the left over food?

Plants prepare their own food. Food is prepared in their leaves.

Some of this food is used up by plants. The left over food is stored in different parts of the plant.

We eat this food. Most of the food we eat comes from plants.

Many plants store food in their fruits.

apples

bananas

mangoes

pineapple

LINKED INTERNET SITES

Learn more about any fruit by clicking on it.
http://www.thefruitpages.com/alphabet.shtml

To the Teacher
Children are already aware that we get fruits, vegetables and foodgrains from plants. We would like them to realise that plants prepare food and store it in various parts—leaves, stems, roots, fruits and seeds.

Some plants store food in their leaves.

cabbage

spinach

coriander

Some plants store food in their stems.

onion

potato

sugarcane

Some plants store food in their roots.

radish

carrot and turnip

Some plants store food in their flowers.

cauliflower

LINKED INTERNET SITES

Learn about fruits and vegetables the fun way!
http://www.dole5aday.com/MusicAndPlay/M_Games.jsp

Plants store food in their seeds for baby plants.
We also eat many of these seeds.

wheat

pea

maize

rice

Remember

1. Plants prepare food. They use up some of the food.
2. The rest of the food is stored in fruits, leaves, stems, roots, flowers and seeds.
3. We eat this food.

Exercises

1. Name these.

(a) A stem that we eat ....

(b) A plant that stores food in its leaves ....

(c) A white coloured root that we eat in salads ....

(d) A seed that we grind to get flour ....

2. Put a ☑ for true, and a ☒ for false.

(a) Plants prepare food in their leaves.

(b) Plants store their extra food only in their fruits.

(c) Plants store food in their seeds for baby plants.

3. What is it — fruit, stem, root, leaf, flower or seed?

(a) banana .... (b) pea .... (c) peach ....

(d) beetroot .... (e) wheat .... (f) sugarcane ....

(g) cabbage .... (h) dal .... (i) apple ....

(j) cauliflower ....

Project

What food does it give us?

In your plant scarp book
write what food each plant gives you.
Remember, all plants do not give you food.
Some give you other things.
We will read about them in the next chapter.

4. Other Uses of Plants

Warming Up!

Look around your home or classroom.
Can you see some things we get from plants?

Plants make the world beautiful

Plants make our world look beautiful.
They beautify our garden and our home.

• Plants clean the air

Smoke from cars and factories makes the air dirty.
Dirty air is bad for our health.
Plants clean the air.
We should plant trees around our house.

• Plants cool the air

Have you noticed that a public park is always cooler than the city?
Plants cool the air and also help in bringing rain.

• Plants give us wood

Wood from plants is used to make chairs, tables, doors and other furniture. Your pencil is made of wood too.

Wood is also used for burning as **fuel**.

To the Teacher
Here we introduce children to the range of products that plants give us. We would also like to inculcate the idea of conservation by showing how our very existence depends on plants.

• Plants give us fibres

The fluffy cotton bolls we get from the cotton plant are used to make cotton fibre. This fibre is used to make cotton clothes.

We get jute fibre from the jute plant. It is used to make sacks, ropes and mats.

cotton

jute

• Plants give us medicines

Several medicines are obtained from plants. Here are some plants that give us medicines.

neem   tulsi   poppy   eucalyptus

• Plants give us perfumes

rose

jasmine

lavender

• Plants give us rubber, paper and gum

Paper is made from bamboo.

Gum is made from the keekar (acasia) tree.

Rubber is made from the rubber tree.

• Plants give us oil

mustard oil

sunflower oil

corn oil

coconut oil

Awareness Science–2

• Plants give us tea, coffee and cocoa

Coffee beans give us coffee.

Tea leaves give us tea.

Seeds of the cocoa tree give us cocoa. Chocolate is made from cocoa.

Remember

1. Plants are useful to us in several ways.
2. They give us many useful things besides food.
3. They also clean and cool the air.

Exercises

1. Name one plant each that gives us these:

   (a) Cooking oil ....

   (b) Fibre for sacks ....

   (c) Perfumes ....

   (d) Gum ....

   (e) Fibre for clothes ....

   (f) Medicine ....

   (g) Paper ....

   (h) Rubber ....

2. Put a ☑ for true, and a ☒ for false.

   (a) Plants make the air around us dirty.

   (b) Plants cool the air.

   (c) Plants help in bringing rain.

3. Why should you plant trees around your house?

   ....

   ....

What do they give us?

1. In your plant scarp book write how each plant is useful to us.

2. Find out from your teacher which fruit tree can grow best where you live.

   Ask your parents to get you the seed or a small plant of the tree.
   Plant the tree near your home.
   Call it your tree. You can also give it a name.
   Take care of it and watch it grow with you.
   In a few years it will start giving you fruits.

3. Explain to other people why trees are important. Encourage them to plant trees.

5. Seeds

When you cut an apple, what do you see in the centre?
How do you think these are useful for the plant?

The small dark brown things in the centre of an apple are the **seeds**.

Other fruits have seeds too. Some fruits have only one seed. Others have several seeds.

A new plant grows from a seed.

apple

peapod

tomato

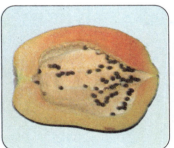

papaya

mango

• Seeds become plants

Most plants grow from seeds.
Seeds have a baby plant inside them.
They also have food for the baby plant.
The baby plant can rest for a long time without growing.
It starts growing when it gets water, air and warmth.

To the Teacher

The objective in this chapter is to strengthen the concept of growth of plants from seeds. Stress the fact that a seed mist become wet before it starts growing, and that the baby plant starts consuming the food only when it starts growing. This concept of dormancy is different from the children's everyday experience of watching animal babies grow, and hence, may be a little difficult for them to grasp.

Soon it grows into a new plant. It grows into a healthy plant if it get water, air, sunshine and good soil.

 **Remember**

1. Fruits have seeds in them.
2. The seed has a baby plant. It also has stored food for the baby plant.
3. A new plant grows from a seed.

 Exercises

1. Put a ☑ for true, and a ☒ for false.

(a) A mango fruit has several seeds in it.

(b) Inside a seed is a baby plant.

(c) When the baby plant starts growing, it has to get its food from outside.

(d) The baby plant can rest in the seed for a long time without growing.

2. What are the things necessary for a baby plant to start growing?

....

....

3. What are the things necessary for a plant to grow well?

....

Project

What do they need?

Take some seeds of bean or gram.
Soak them overnight in water.
Take three dishes and keep some wet cotton in them.

Put a few seeds in all the dishes.
Keep dish 1 in the kitchen. Keep the cotton wet by adding water if it dries.

In dish 2 add enough water to drown the seeds. They will not get air.

Keep dish 3 in the refrigerator. The seeds will not get warmth.

In which dish did the baby plants start growing? Why?

Revision Test Paper-1

1. Fill in the blanks.

   (a) The stem of a tree is called the ....

   (b) Plants that need support to climb up are called ....

   (c) Plants store food in their .... for baby plants.

   (d) A baby plant in a seed starts growing when it
        gets .... , ... , and ....

2. Match the following.

   (a) Herbs   (i)   Deserts

   (b) Cactus   (ii) Live for few months only

   (c) Onion   (iii) A stem with food stored in it

   (d) Fruits   (iv) Made from bamboo

   (e) Paper   (v)   Seeds

3. Name the four kinds of plants. Give one example of each.

   ....

   ....

4. In which part of the plant is food prepared? ....

5. Name three plant parts where food is stored. Give one example of

   each. ....

   ....

6. What do the following plants give us?

   jute ....   neem ....

   keekar (acasia) ....   sunflower ....

7. What things does a plant need to grow well?

   ....

8. In your note book draw the diagram of a baby plant growing from a
   seed.

6. Animals – Their body structures

Warming Up!

A bear is an animal. Whale is a fish.
Think! In what ways are they different from each other?

There are several types of animals on the earth.
They are of different shapes and sizes.
They live in different places. Some live on land. Some live in water.
Some can live on both land and water. Some animals can fly.
They eat different kinds of food.

The body structures of animals are suitable for the places they live in and the food they eat.

• Where animals live

polar bear

fish

Fishes live in water. They have **fins** instead of legs. Fins help them to swim.

They have **gills** that help them breathe under water.

Polar bears live in very cold places. They have a lot of **fur** on their body. It protects them from cold.

To the Teacher

After recapitulating a little of what the children learnt in Book 1, we cover, in short, the concept of adaptation in animals without giving any terminology. While most children will be aware that the body structures of different animals differ, they would have associated only the most obvious, such as wings, to their lifestyle.

Birds have very light bodies.

They have **feathers** on their bodies.

They have **wings** that help them to fly.

bird

frog

Frogs live on both land and water.

They have **webbed feet** which help them to swim.

Camels live in hot and dry deserts, where there is very little food and water.

They can go without food and water for months.

They have a **hump** in which certain kind of food is stored.

camel

• What animals eat

Animals having different eating habits also differ in their body structure.

Some animals eat the flesh of other animals. They have **claws** and **sharp teeth** to tear the flesh.

lion

Animals that eat plants do not have claws.

They have **flat teeth** to chew the plants.

cow

An elephant uses its trunk to break leaves and put them in its mouth.
A giraffe has a long neck. With its help, it can eat leaves of tall trees.

elephant

giraffe

kingfisher

Some bird such as kingfisher have long beaks.
They use their beaks to catch fish.

LINKED INTERNET SITES

Participate in a quiz to see how much you know about body structures of different kinds of animals.
http://www.ecokids.ca/pub/eco_info/topics/climate/adaptations/index.cfm

• How animals protect themselves

Some animals have body parts they use to protect themselves.

deer

tortoise

eel

Cows, deer and many other animals have horns.
A tortoise has a thick body covering. It hides beneath it when there is danger.
An electric eel gives an electric shock to anyone touching it.

Remember

1. Animals living in different places, differ in their body structure.
2. Animals having different eating habits differ in their body structure.
3. Some animals have body parts that they use to protect themselves from enemies.

Exercises

1. How does each of these help the animal?

(a) Fur on the body ....

(b) The hump of camels ....

(c) Sharp teeth ....

(d) Fins ....

(e)   The long neck of a giraffe ....

(f)   An elephant's trunk ....

(g)   The thick body covering of a tortoise ....
....

(h)   The horns of a cow ....

(i)   The beak of a kingfisher ....

2. **Put a ☑ for true, and a ☒ for false.**

(a) Birds have light bodies. ☐

(b) Frogs always live in water, like fishes. ☐

(c) The electric eel can be easily caught. ☐

(d) If a tortoise sees danger, it hides inside its shell. ☐

Project

Make an animal scarp book

Collect picture of animals. Paste them in a scarp book.
Below each picture write

(a)   its name

(b)   where it is normally found

(c)   how it protects itself

(d)   what kind of home it makes for itself

(e)   where it lives

(f)   how it moves

(g)   what it eats

Give two pages to each animal.
Leave blank spaces for things
you do not know. You will be
able to fill them up later, as you learn more about animals.

7. Wild Animals

Warming Up!

Have you ever seen a tiger or a bear around your house?
Where do you think they live?

Some animals live in jungles. They are **wild animals**.

tiger

zebra

bear

Have you seen wild animals in the zoo?
Do you think it is right to keep them in cages?

• What they eat

Some wild animals eat plants.

elephant

deer

rabbit

To the Teacher

Our effort here is to also make children aware of the need for conservation of wild life. The project in this chapter is also geared towards this aim. The rest of the chapter is more or less repetition of what they read in Book 1, for reinforcing the concepts.

Some wild animals hunt other animals. They eat their flesh.

lions attacking a buffalo

wolf

crocodile

Some animals eat the dead bodies of other animals.
They help to keep the jungle clean.

hyenas and vultures eating a dead animal

jackal

• Where they live

Some animals build their own homes.

Rabbits make burrows to live in

Birds make nests to live in

A spider makes a web.

Some animals find a place to live in. An owl finds a hole in a tree.

Some animals such as elephants or wolves do not have a home. They wander around in the jungle.

• Animals in danger

Today humans are cutting trees in jungles for wood, and to make cities. This is bad for us. Can you say why?

It is bad for the animals also. They are being driven out of their homes.

We are also killing wild animals for their skin, which gives leather.

We kill rabbits and other animals for their fur to make clothes.

We kill elephants for their tusks, which is used to make ivory.

Because of all this, the number of animals in our world is reducing. We should not allow this to happen. We should protect animals.

LINKED INTERNET SITES

Play animal games. http://resources.kaboose.com/games/animals2.html

Remember

1. Wild animals live in jungles.
2. Wild animals have different eating habits.
3. Some wild animals build their own homes. Other find a place to live in.
4. We should protect wild animals.

Exercises

1. Complete the table.

Animal	What it eats
a. Rabbit	....
b. Lion	....
c. Deer	....
d. Hyena	....

2. Complete the table.

Animal	Where it lives
a. Rabbit	....
b. Owl	....
c. Spider	....
d. Elephant	....

3. For which body parts are these animals killed?

(a) Elephants:.................................... (b) Snakes:....................................

(c) Rabbits:.................................... (d) Crocodiles:....................................

4. Discuss in class and answer.

What do you think will happen if we kill all animals that eat the dead bodies of other animals?

....

....

Project

What is their use?

Are you afraid of the snake? Do you think that it is a useless animal?
But imagine what would happen if all snakes were killed.
Then, there would be nobody to kill rats.
There would be too many rats.
They will eat up all your grain.
They will ruin all your books and clothes.
You would, then, have to call a pied piper to kill the rats!
So, after all, snakes are useful too.
So are most other animals.

8. Domestic Animals

Some animals can be tamed.

We keep them in our houses or in farms.

They are **domestic animals**.

They are very useful to us.

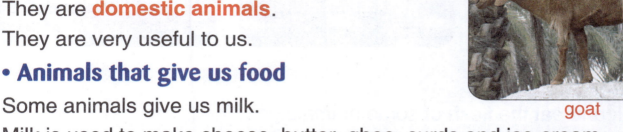
goat

• Animals that give us food

Some animals give us milk.

Milk is used to make cheese, butter, ghee, curds and ice-cream.

cow

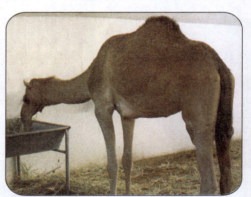
camel

buffalo

milk products

To the Teacher

Here is an excellent opportunity to create awareness among children for the need to prevent cruelty towards animals. Explain that a number of people are becoming vegetarians and are refusing to wear silk or leather because they feel we have no right to be cruel to animals.

Some animals give us eggs.

hen   eggs   duck

We cook and eat the flesh of some animals.

hen   duck   sheep

goat   crab   fish

• Animals that give us other things

Some animals give us fibres which we use to make clothes.

Sheep gives us wool

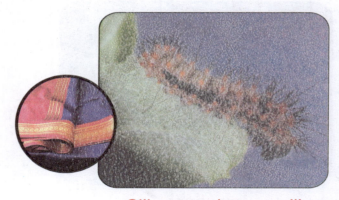

Silkworm gives us silk

Leather is made from the skin of some domestic and wild animals.
Leather is used to make shoes, clothes, purses, belts and other things.

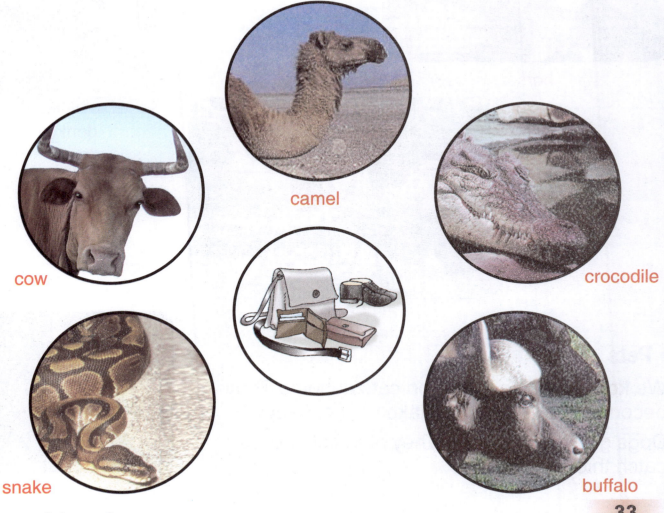

camel

cow

crocodile

snake

buffalo

• Animals that carry loads for us

Some animals carry loads for us.

elephant

bullock

horse

donkey

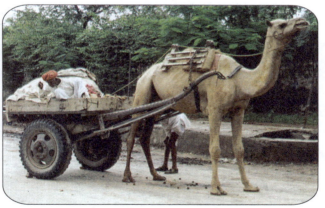

camel

• Pets

We keep pets like dogs and cats at home. They become our friends and make us feel happy.

Dogs guard our homes. They also help police catch thieves.

dog

Animals are our friends. They give us many things.
We should be kind to them. We should look after them well.

 **LINKED INTERNET SITES**

Visit a farm – see and hear the farm animals.
http://www.kidsfarm.com/farm.htm

 **Remember**

1. We keep domestic animals in our house and in farms.
2. Domestic animals are very useful to us.
3. They give us food, fibre and leather.
4. They carry loads for us.

 Exercises

1. Complete the table. Write one way in which the animal is useful to us.

	Animal	Domestic or wild	How it is useful to us
(a)	Cow	....	....
(b)	Dog	....	....
(c)	Hen	....	....
(d)	Goat	....	....
(e)	Snake	....	....
(f)	Silkworm	....	....
(g)	Camel	....	....

2. Why should you be kind to animals? ....

....

Project

Prevent cruelty to animals

Have you ever thrown stones at a dog? Do you think it is right?

You should not be cruel to animals.

If you see someone being cruel to animals, stop him.

Explain to him why we should not be cruel to animals.

Make the following table in your exercise book and complete it.

HOW I PREVENTED CRUELTY TO ANIMALS

Name of person	Cruelty shown	Did he or she agree not to do it again

9. Other Animals

• Insects

Insects are small animals. They have six legs.
Some of them have **wings**, and can fly.
Some of them have **feelers** on their heads.
They can feel with them like we can feel with our hands.

butterfly

Some insects have a pipe in their mouth, instead of teeth. They suck our blood or nectar of flowers with it, like you drink cold drink with a straw!

mosquito

cockroach

ladybird

grasshopper

LINKED INTERNET SITES

Learn about insects.
http://www.urbanext.uiuc.edu/insects/index.html

• Birds

Birds have **feathers** on their bodies. They have very light bodies. They have **wings** instead of hands. All these help in flying. But some birds such as penguin and kiwi cannot fly.

owl

To the Teacher
The purpose of this chapter is to introduce children to the diversity of life, especially underwater life, which many of them will be less familiar with.

penguin

kiwi

vulture

Most birds make nests in trees. The female bird lays eggs in the nest. Baby birds hatch out of these eggs.

● Fishes and other water animals

Many kinds of animals live in water. Some live in ponds, lakes and rivers. Others live in the salty water of the sea.

The bodies of most water animals are shaped like boats. This helps them to swim fast in water.

crab

shark

seahorse

lobster

fish

whale

octopus

Some water animals like fish breathe through their gills.
They breathe inside water. They breathe air dissolved in water.

Others such as whales have to come up to the surface of water to breathe.

LINKED INTERNET SITES

Take print outs of animals living in or near water for colouring.
http://www.childstoryhour.com/coloringanimal.htm
Make an octopus using the instructions and printouts from the site.
http://www.dltk-kids.com/animals/moctopus.html

Remember

1. Insects are small animals with six legs.
2. Birds have feathers on their bodies. Most of them can fly.
3. Several kinds of animals live inside water.

Exercises

1. Put a ☑ for true and a ☒ for false.

(a) No animal can live in the salty water of the sea.
(b) The mosquito bites us with its teeth.
(c) All water animals can breathe inside water.
(d) Insects cannot fly.
(e) Baby birds hatch out of eggs.

2. Why are bodies of fishes shaped like boats?..

....

3. How are baby birds born? ....

....

Project

1. Include insects, birds and water animals in your animal scrap book.

2. Study eating habits of birds.

Take two dishes. Put water in one dish, and some wheat or rice grains in the other.

Keep the dishes in a quiet place outside your house near a tree.

Stand quietly in a corner, and watch the birds eat and drink.

Find out the names of the birds. Include them in your scarp book. Change the food in the dish every day. You can try fruit and vegetable pieces, meat pieces, sugar, dals or beans. Note which food they eat and which food they do not eat.

Revision Test Paper-2

1. Fill in the blanks:

(a) A cow has .... teeth to chew grass and other plants.

(b) The .... has a thick body covering that protects it from enemies.

(c) .... and .... do not live in homes.

(d) Leather shoes and belts are made from the .... of some animals.

(e) Fishes breathe through their ....

2. Match the following:

(a) Polar bear   (i) Eats dead bodies of animals

(b) Flesh-eating animals   (ii) Wool

(c) Hyena   (iii) Fur on body

(d) Sheep   (iv) Insects

(e) Feelers   (v) Claws and sharp teeth

3. How does the electric eel protect itself from its enemies?.................

....

4. Name two animals that help in keeping the jungle clean.....................

....

5. Name two animals that carry loads for us. ....

....

6. How are feelers useful to insects? ....

....

7. Why are bodies of most fish shaped like boats? ....

....

10. Air

Warming Up!

Hold a piece of paper in front of a running fan. What makes the paper move? Stand outside on a windy day. What makes the leaves, your hair and your clothes move? Can you see that thing?

• Air is all round you.

Air is all around you. But you cannot see it. You can only feel air when it moves. Moving air is called **wind**.

LINKED INTERNET SITES

Make a wind streamer.
http://bird.miamisci.org/hurricane/windstreamer.html

Push an empty glass upside down into water. The water does not enter the glass. Why? Because the glass is full of air.

You have to take the air out of the glass. Tilt the glass in the water. Air bubbles will come out of the glass.
Water can now enter the glass.

To the Teacher

Since children cannot see air, it is a little difficult for them to understand that air is everywhere. We have, therefore, thought it necessary to repeat the important concepts about air, which have earlier been covered in Book 1.

The space around you is not empty. It is full of air.

• Air fills things

Blow air into a balloon. Why does it become bigger?
It becomes filled with air.

You can blow air into things using a bicycle pump.

• Air has weight

Which is heavier? A football full of air or an empty football?

A football full of air is heavier.
The air inside it has weight.

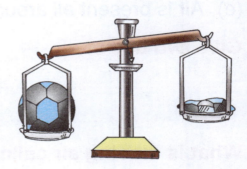

• Air is needed for burning

Air is needed to burn things.
Cover a burning candle with a glass tumbler.
It stops burning after some time.
It needs more air to keep on burning.

• Air is needed for breathing

We breathe air all the time. It keeps us alive. All plants and animals breathe air.

We need clean air to breathe. Dirty air is bad for our health.

Remember

1. The space around you has air.
2. We can fill things with air.
3. Air has weight.
4. Air is needed for burning.
5. We need clean air to breathe.

Exercises

1. Put a ☑ for true and ☒ for false.

(a) We cannot see air. We can only feel it when it moves.

(b) Air does not have weight.

(c) Air is needed for burning.

(d) If we breathe dirty air, we can become ill.

(e) Air is present all around us.

2. Give two use of air.

....

....

3. What is moving air called? ....

4. When you blow into a balloon, what does it get filled with?

....

 Project

Make things that float in air.

A **parachute** is like a large balloon. With its help you can jump out of an airplane flying high up. You will slowly float down to the ground!

You can build a small parachute with just a handkerchief, string and a stone.

- Tie four pieces of string to the four corners of a handkerchief.
- Tie the other ends of the strings to a small stone.

Your parachute is ready.

Drop it from a height, and watch it float down!

11. What does Air Have?

• Air has gases

Air has several **gases**. Some of them are very useful for us. But some gases given out by cars and factories are harmful.

When they mix in the air, the air becomes dirty.

harmful gases are given out by cars, buses and factories

• Air has dust particles

Look carefully at sunlight coming into your room from a window.

Can you see small particles of **dust** in the air?

• Air has smoke

Smoke is given out when something burns.

It gets mixed in the air. It makes the air dirty.

It is harmful for us.

Awareness Science–2

• Air has water vapour

When you hang wet clothes in the sun, they become dry.

What happens to the water in the clothes?

Water changes to form a gas, which cannot be seen. It is called **water vapour**. It gets mixed with the air.

Water from seas, rivers, lakes and ponds keeps changing into water vapour, because of the heat of the sun. Thus, air has water vapour.

• Air has germs

Air also has a number of very small living things which cannot be seen.

Some of them are harmful to us. If they get inside our body, they can make us ill.

They are called **germs**.

We need clean and pure air for breathing. Dirty and impure air is harmful for us.

Dust, smoke and harmful gases make the air dirty and impure.

Plants clean the air.

LINKED INTERNET SITES

Do an experiment to find out how much the air around you is polluted.
http://www.scapca.org/pollution_check-up.asp

Remember

1. Air has several gases.
2. Air has dust particles.
3. Air has water vapour.
4. Air has smoke which is harmful for us.
5. Air has germs which can make us ill.

Exercises

1. Put a ☑ for true and ☒ for false.

(a) All gases in the air are harmful. ☐

(b) We can see dust particles in the air. ☐

(c) Smoke and harmful gases are given out by cars and factories. ☐

(d) Germs are very harmful to us. ☐

(e) Air with lots of dust, smoke or harmful gases is bad for our health. ☐

(f) More water vapour gets into air in summer than in winter. ☐

2. How does water vapour get into air? ....

....

3. Name the things that air contains. ....

....

Project

Dip two handkerchiefs of the same size in water.

Squeeze them to remove some water.
Put one of them in the sun.
Put the other in the shade of a tree.
Check how much they have dried after every 10 minutes.
Which handkerchief dries first?
What do you conclude?

12. The Wind

Air around us can move from one place to another. You already know that moving air is called wind. Moving air makes these things work.

kite

windmill

sailboat

hang glider

Sometimes the wind blows slowly. It is called **breeze**.

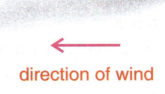

direction of wind

You can find the direction in which the wind is blowing.

Take some dust in your hands. On releasing the dust, it gets blown in the direction of the wind.

48

When the wind blows fast, it is called a **gale**.
Strong gales can even uproot trees.
They can cause a lot of damage.

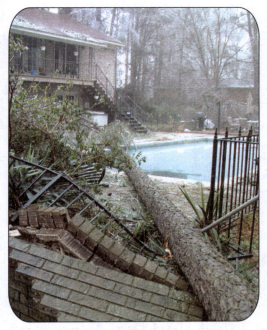

damage caused by gale

A **wind vane** tells us the direction of the wind.

a windvane

An instrument like the one shown here can be used to measure the speed of the wind.

The wind spins the cups.
When the wind blows fast, the cups also spin fast.

LINKED INTERNET SITES

Wind and rain projects for kids (teacher/parent help required): Go to
http://www.learningkids.com/experiments.asp and click on 'Wind and Rain.

Remember

1. When wind blows slowly, it is called breeze.
2. When wind blows very fast, it is called gale.
3. A wind vane tells us the direction of wind.

Exercises

1. Name these :

   (a) Moving air. ....

   (b) Gentle wind. ....

   (c) Very strong wind. ....

   (d) It tells us the direction of wind. ....

2. How can you say that wind has a lot of force? ....

....

3. If you did not have a wind vane, how would you find the direction

   of wind? ....

   ....

   ....

4. Name three things which work because of wind. ....

   ....

   ....

 ─LINKED INTERNET SITES────────────

Read an online book about the wind - click on 'Watch the wind'.
http://www.kizclub.com/Sbody.html

Make a wind vane

Cut two pieces from a chart paper in the shape shown (triangle).
Cut slits at the two ends of a plastic drinking straw.
Insert the two card triangles into the slits,
to get the shape of an arrow.
If they do not stay in place use a tape.
Take a pencil which has a rubber at one end.
Make it stand upright on a piece of a plasticine.
Push a drawing pin through the centre of the
straw.
Then push it into the rubber on the pencil.
Your wind vane is ready for use.
Put it outside. It will point in the direction of the wind.

13. Water

Warming Up!

How do you feel if you do not get water to drink for a long time?
Do you think you can live without water?

We need water to live. We cannot live for more than a few days without water. Plants and animals also need water to live.

Besides drinking, we need water for many other things. Can you make a list of such things?

• Where do we get water from?

Water comes from rain. Some of this water goes under the soil. It collects deep down in the earth. We can bring out this water by digging wells and tubewells.

Rain water also fills up lakes, rivers and ponds.

To the Teacher

Most children love to play with water. They already know a lot about water, and its properties. Some of them may even be aware of the three states in which water can exist. Important concepts to be got across to them are that water, even if it looks clean may contain germs, and can be the cause of many diseases, and that they should not waste potable water.

River water flows into the sea.

In most parts of India we get rain from June to September. During other months there is not much rain. Many rivers therefore dry up.

We store river water by making **dams** which hold water in **reservoirs**. **Canals** supply water from rivers and reservoirs to far off places.

a dam

Water from lakes, rivers or ponds is not clean enough to drink. It contains dirt and germs.

Dirty water from our homes and factories also flows into rivers. This makes the river water even more dirty.

If you drink dirty water, it can make you ill.

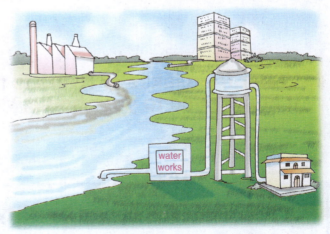

Water has to be cleaned before supplying to our homes. The dirt has to be removed and the germs have to be killed. This is done in the **waterworks** in your city.

Clean water is precious. You should not waste it.

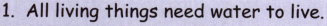

1. All living things need water to live.
2. Water comes from rain.
3. Rain water fills up lakes, rivers and ponds.
4. We build dams to store water.
5. Drinking dirty water can make us ill. Water is cleaned before it is supplied to our homes.

Exercises

1. Put a ☑ for true and a ☒ for false.

(a) Only some living things need water to live.

(b) River water flows into the sea.

(c) Dams prevent river water from flowing away.

(d) Water that looks clean will not have any germs in it.

2. If you dig deep into the earth, you can get water. Why? ....

....

....

3. How does water from homes and factories make the river dirty?

....

....

4. Water from lakes or rivers is first taken to the waterworks before it is supplied to your home. Why? ....

....

Project

Diseases caused by dirty water

Germs in water cause a number of dangerous diseases. Make a list of such diseases by asking your teacher and parents.

Check with a doctor how he or she finds out if a person has any of these diseases. Ask how each of these can be cured.

14. Forms of Water

What happens when water is kept in the freezer of a refrigerator?
It becomes very cold and then it changes into ice.
If you keep the ice outside, it melts to form water again.

Ice is hard. You can hold it in your hand. It is a **solid**.

Water can flow. It can be poured. It is a **liquid**.
Ice is also water. It is water in the solid form.

If you heat water, it starts boiling. If you keep on heating it, its quantity reduces. Why?

On heating, water changes into a gas called **steam** or **water vapour**. When water changes into steam or water vapour, we say that it has **evaporated**.

If you keep a cool steel plate over the boiling water, you will see tiny drops of water on it. Where did this water come from?

It came from steam. When steam is cooled, it changes back to water.

To the Teacher

By illustrating the three forms of matter through water, ice and steam, with which children are most familiar, we have here generalized the concept to all matter. Children should not have any problems in grasping this, and in realising the differences in the three states. The children may have difficulty in understanding that as you go higher up in the atmosphere, it gets cooler. They may argue that it should become hotter since you are getting closer to the Sun! Explain that air cannot absorb much heat directly from the Sun.

Thus, steam is also another form of water. It is the gas form of water. Gases can spread out everywhere. Most of them cannot be seen.

• The Water Cycle

You know that on heating, water changes into water vapour. Water vapour on cooling changes back into water. This happens in nature also.

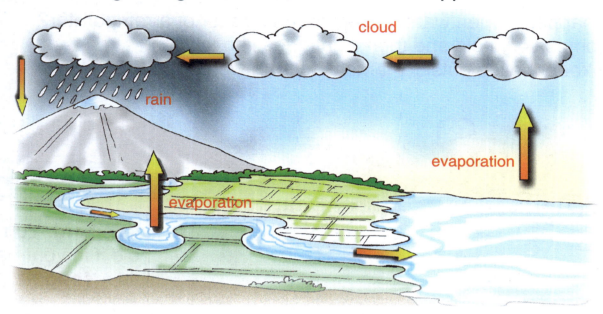

Water in the seas, lakes, rivers, ponds or streams evaporates because of the heat of the sun.

The water vapour rises up. The air higher up is cool. This cools the water vapour. It forms tiny drops of water.

Many such drops of water together form a **cloud**.
When the clouds pass through cooler air, they get further cooled.
The water drops then become bigger.
When clouds become too heavy with water, rain falls.

This rain water again goes into oceans, rivers, lakes, ponds and streams. It again evaporates. This goes on repeating again and again.

Thus, the **water cycle** in nature goes on and on.

— LINKED INTERNET SITES —

Games and activities on the water cycle.
http://www.epa.gov/safewater/kids/kids_k-3.html

56

• Hail and snow

Sometimes, when it is very cold high up, water drops freeze to form ice on their way down.

They then come down as **hail**.

Sometimes, water drops freeze while still in the clouds, and come down as **snow**.

hailstones are small balls of ice

a snowflake is beautiful, every snowflake has a different design

Remember

1. Ice, water and steam are different forms of water.
2. The water on the earth evaporates to form water vapour. This forms clouds as it goes up. Clouds bring rain and the water comes down to the earth again. This is called the water cycle.
3. Sometimes, when it is very cold high up, water freezes to form hail or snow.

Exercises

1. Is heating or cooling required to carry out this change? Write H for heating and C for cooling on top of the arrows.

(a) Ice --------→ water

(b) Water-------→ ice

(c) Water ------→ steam

(d) Steam -------→ water

2. Name the form of water.

(a) It is hard. You can hold it in your hand: ....

(b) It flows and can be poured: ....

(c) It cannot be seen: ....

3. Put a ☑ for true, and a ☒ for false.

(a) The air high up is hotter.

(b) Clouds contains tiny drops of water.

(c) When drops of water freeze on their way down from the clouds they form hailstones.

(d) Water evaporates only when it is boiled.

(e) When water freezes in the clouds, if forms snow.

4. Fill in the blanks.

Project

Dissolving in Water

Take water in three glass tumblers.

Put a teaspoonful of sugar in one tumbler, a teaspoonful of sand in the second tumbler, and a teaspoonful of salt in the third tumbler.

Stire the water in all the glasses.

Out of the three things added, which one have dissolved in water? Try this out with other solids. Complete the table:

Name of solid	Whether it dissolves in water	Name of solid	Whether it dissolves in water
1. Salt		4. Wheat	
2. Sugar		5. Rice	
3. Sand		6. Coffee powder	

Revision Test Paper-3

1. Fill in the blanks:

(a) All plants and animals need .... to breathe.

(b) Very small harmful living beings present in air are called ....

(c) A .... tells us the direction of air.

(d) Before supplying water to our homes, it is cleaned in the ....

(e) Ice is the .... form of water.

2. Match the following:

(a) Burning   (i)   Water vapour

(b) Water cycle   (ii) Can uproot trees

(c) Gale   (iii) Air

(d) Dam   (iv) Water---→ water vapour ---→ clouds---→ rain

(e) Evaporation   (v)   Reservoir to hold water

3. Give two uses of air ....
....

4. Name three things that air contains. ....
....

5. What is the difference between breeze and gale?...............................
....

6. Water is present deep down in the earth. How can we use this water?
....
....

7. How can you change

(a) Ice to water ....

(b) Steam to water ....

8. Why do clouds form high up in the sky?...
....

15. The Sun, Moon, Stars and the Earth

• The Sun and stars

The Sun is a huge ball of fire. It is very far away from us. It gives us heat and light.

Without the Sun, the Earth would have been very cold and dark. We would not be able to live on it.

The stars are also huge balls of fire. In fact the Sun is also a star. It is the star closest to the Earth.

60

The other stars are very far away. That is why they appear so small. It will take a rocket thousands of years to reach the next nearest star!

• The Earth

The Sun, the Moon, and the stars are shaped like balls. The Earth on which we live is also shaped like a ball.

Do you find this difficult to believe? You feel it is flat because it is a very big ball.

But if you fly in an aeroplane in one direction only, you would come back to the place where you started.

It will take you about two days to fly around the Earth.

The men who went to the Moon saw the Earth from there. It looked like a big, round, shining ball.

earth

earth from moon

• The Moon

The Moon is the smallest and the nearest object in the sky.
But it is much further away than the clouds.

The Moon does not give out its own light. It shines when the light of the Sun falls on it.

Moon

• Day and night

The Earth spins round and round.
But you cannot feel it going round and round.
This is because everything on the Earth goes around with the Earth.
The air also moves with the Earth.

Do you know that when it is day in India, it is night in America?

When India faces towards the Sun, America is facing away from it. Now when the Earth spins around, it becomes night in India and day in America.

As the Earth continues spinning, day and night follow each other.

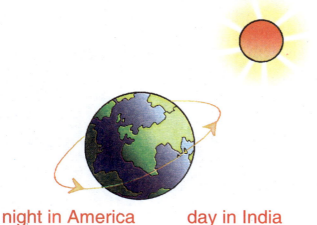

night in America   day in India   night in India   day in America

Night and day occur because the Earth spins round and round.

LINKED INTERNET SITES

Read an online book about the sky – click on 'What's in the sky?'
http://www.kizclub.com/Sbody.html

Remember

1. Stars are huge balls of fire. The Sun is also a star.
2. The Earth is shaped like a ball.
3. The Moon is our nearest neighbour in space.
4. The Earth spins round and round. This causes day and night.

Exercises

1. Put a ☑ for true and a ☒ for false.

(a) All stars give out heat and light.

(b) The Sun is the star closest to the Earth.

(c) The Moon is bigger than the Sun.

(d) The Moon gives out its own light.

(e) There is life on the Earth because of the Sun.

2. Fill in the blanks with the correct answer.

(a) The Earth is .... (flat/round)

(b) The Earth moves ....
(in a straight line/round and round)

(c) It is .... on the side of the Earth facing away from the Sun. (day/night)

(d) It is .... on the side of the Earth facing the Sun. (day/night)

3. What causes day and night on the Earth? ....

....

Heating with the Sun

You know that the Sun heats up the Earth.
The heat of the Sun can be used to do useful
things. It can be used to heat water.
Take two small tin boxes. Colour one of
them black.

Take water in both. Keep both of them
outside in bright sunshine. After two
hours dip your fingers in both. In which
box has the water become warmer?
Black coloured things take in
more heat than others.

Why are water heaters which use the Sun's heat coloured black?

16. Light and Shadows

Warming Up!

Why can't you see properly when it is dark? Think! What is missing at that time?

• Light

The Sun gives us light. Some other things also give us light. A glowing electric bulb and a burning candle give us light.

A table or a book does not give out light. The Sun, the electric bulb and the candle are **sources of light**.

sources of light

We can see things like a book or a table because of light from these sources of light.

If you throw a ball towards a wall it bounces off. When light strikes anything, it also bounces off. We call this **reflection of light**.

When anything reflects light to our eyes, we can see that thing.

To the Teacher

The key concept with which children may have difficulty is that of reflection of light and the fact that we see things when they reflect light to our eyes. Showing them torch light being reflected by a mirror in a dark room will help to reinforce the concept.

sunlight reflected by a mirror

• Shadows

Have you seen your shadow on the ground while standing in sunlight?

Have you ever made shadow figures on the wall, using the light of an electric bulb?

A shadow is formed when the path of light is blocked by something. When you stand in sunlight, your shadow looks like you.

But sometimes it is short and sometimes it is long.
It is short at noon when the Sun is right above your head. It is long in the morning and evening.

As the Sun moves in the sky, the shadow also changes direction.

morning shadow afternoon shadow evening shadow

There were no clocks in olden days.
People used the direction of the shadow of a pole to tell the time of the day.
This is called a **sun dial**.

a sun dial

LINKED INTERNET SITES

Fun experiments with shadows :
http://www.bbc.co.uk/schools/scienceclips/ages/7_8/light_shadows.shtml

Remember

1. The Sun, the electric bulb or a candle are sources of light.
2. If anything reflects light to our eyes, we can see that thing.
3. A shadow is formed when the path of light is blocked by some object.

Exercises

1. Put a ☑ for true and a ☒ for false.

(a) Sun and stars are sources of light.

(b) If no light falls on this book, you can still see it.

(c) You see things when they reflect light towards your eyes.

(d) Whenever the path of light is blocked by an object, a shadow of the object is formed.

(e) Your shadow formed by the Sun does not change throughout the day.

(f) We can use a sun dial to tell the time at night.

2. Name these

(a) Three sources of light: .... , ... , ...

(b) Bouncing off of light: ....

(c) It is formed when light is blocked by an object: ....

3. In which case do you think the shadow will be longer? Try out and see for yourself.

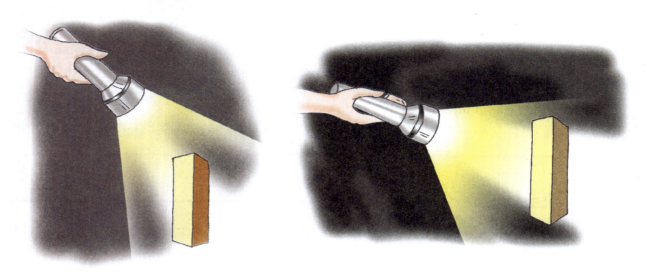

Project

Make your own sun dial

You will need a pencil, a sheet of card paper, and some plasticine. Cut a large circle from the card. Place the plasticine in the centre of the card. Fix the pencil on the plasticine so that it stands straight.

Your sun dial is ready. Keep it in the Sun. The shadow of the pencil falls on the card. The position and the length of the shadow change during the day.

Trace the shadow of the pencil on the card after every hour.

Write the time against each shadow.

You can now use your sun dial to tell the time.

Revision Test Paper-4

1. Fill in the blanks.

(a) The Sun is the .... closest to the Earth.

(b) The shape of the Earth is like a ....

(c) The spinning of the Earth causes .... and ....

(d) We can see this book because it .... light to our eyes.

(e) The Sun is a .... of light.

2. Match the following:

(a) Stars closest to Earth   (i) Reflection

(b) Blocking of light   (ii) Moon

(c) Our closest neighbour in the sky   (iii) Shadow

(d) Bouncing off of light   (iv) Sun

3. Arrange these according to their distances from the Earth. Put the nearest first: Sun, Moon, clouds, stars other than the Sun.

....

4. Could we live on the Earth if there was no Sun? Why?

....

....

5. The Earth does not give out its own light. But it shines when seen from the Moon. Why?

....

....

6. We cannot see anything in a dark room. But if we light a bulb in the dark room we can see everything. Why? ....

....

....

7. When is a shadow formed? ....

....

17. What are Things Made of?

Some things around you are made of **wood**. We get wood from trees.

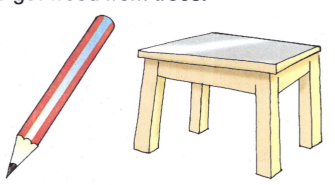

Some things are made of **plastics**. Plastics are made in factories. Plastics are of many types. Some are hard. Some are soft. They come in different colours.

To the Teacher

It is not so important for students to remember what each thing is made of. It is more important for them to know why things are made from certain substances and not from others. The stress should therefore be on why materials are appropriate for certain uses and not for others. A discussion in class about the use of alternate materials to make certain things will be very useful. Let the children give their own ideas on which material is best and why.

Many things are made of **metals**.
They are hard and shiny.
They do not break easily. They do not catch fire.
We get metals from the earth.
Iron and aluminium are common metals.

Some things are made of leather. **Leather** is made from skins of animals.

Some things are made of **glass**. We can see through glass. Light can pass through glass. Glass is made from sand. Glass can break easily.

Cloth is made from **fibres**.
Cotton fibre is obtained from plants.
Wool and silk are obtained from animals.

Rubber bands, tyres and tubes are some things made from **rubber**.
Rubber can be stretched and bent easily.
Rubber is made from a liquid collected from the rubber tree.

 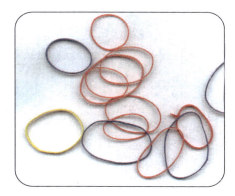 

This book is made from **paper**. Paper is made out of wood.

Paper is thin. We can tear it easily.

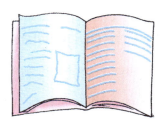

Remember

1. Things around us are made from different materials.
2. Some materials are hard, some are soft, some can be stretched easily.

Exercises

1. **What will you use to make these things? Discuss the reasons in class.**
   (a) Bulbs and tubelights. ....
   (b) Cooking utensils. ....
   (c) Knives. ....
   (d) Window panes. ....

2. **Why will you not make**
   (a) doors in your house of glass? ....
   ....
   (b) clothes hanger of rubber? ....
   ....
   (c) clothes from paper? ....
   ....
   (d) cricket bat from leather? ....
   ....
   (e) hammer from rubber? ....
   ....

3. **List one thing each made out of the following. Can it be made of something else also?**

		What else can it be made of?
(a) metal	....	....
(b) wood	....	....
(c) plastic	....	....
(d) leather	....	....
(e) rubber	....	....

18. Our Houses

A house gives us shelter. It protects us from the sun, rain or snow, and wind. People live in different types of houses.
They use different types of materials for their house.

Most of us live in houses made out of bricks, cement and steel.
We use wood and glass for the doors and windows.

steel

wood

bricks

cement

glass

materials used to build houses

To the Teacher

Stress should be laid on how climatic condition affect the structure of the house. Do point out how much it costs to build different types of houses and hence show why in India a number of people still live in kuchha houses.

Take this opportunity to introduce building materials. A visit to a building site would be useful in showing how steel is used to provide strength to the structure - an understanding of this would be used later to introduce the function of the skeleton in the human body. Bricks can be likened to cells in the body.

a pucca house   a multistorey building   flats

houses made of steel, wood, cement, bricks and glass

These houses cost a lot of money.

Many people use other things such as
mud, straw, wood and even snow to make their houses.
These houses are not so expensive.

a house made of mud and straw

a house made of wood

a house made of snow

A house made of snow is called an **igloo**. It is made by Eskimos
who live in very cold places. There is snow throughout the year in
these places.

Some people do not stay in one place. They keep moving about. They make houses which can be taken from one places to another.

Some of them can move on wheels. Other can float on water. Some houses can be easily folded and carried along.

It is also easy to put up such houses.

camper

house boat

tent

houses that can be carried along

Roofs of house can be flat or sloping.

Flat roofs can be used in various ways. But in a place where it rains or snow very much, water and snow can collect on flat roofs. This can damage the roofs.

Houses in such places have sloping roofs.

sloping roofs

LINKED INTERNET SITES

Read about research on different types of houses done by children
http://www.schools.ash.org.au/elanorah/homes.htm

Remember

1. A house gives us shelter.
2. Most houses in cities are made of bricks, cement and steel.
3. Some houses can be moved from one place to another.
4. In places where it rains or snows a lot, houses have sloping roofs.

Exercises

1. Put a ☑ for true and a ☒ for false.

(a) House made of straw and mud are very strong. ☐

(b) Some people carry their houses with them. ☐

(c) Water and snow can collect on sloping roofs. ☐

(d) House made out of steel, bricks and cement are very expensive. ☐

2. Are there houses made out of snow in India also? Give reasons.

....

....

3. What do you think are the materials used to build your house?

....

....

4. Name the following:

(a) A house made of snow. ....

(b) A house that can float on a river. ....

(c) A house that can be folded and carried along. ....

Project

Ask your parents or your teacher to take you to a place where a pucca house is being built. Make a list of the materials being used. Make a list of the tools and machines being used.

See how steel rods are used to make the house strong.

See how cement is used to join together bricks to make the walls.

Ask the builder how he makes the roof strong.

19. Rocks

Collect different types of rocks. Wash them and look at them carefully. Observe their colour and smoothness. See which ones are easier to break.

The earth is made up of rocks and soil. There are different kinds of rocks. They are of various shapes and sizes. They have different colours.

Some rocks are very hard.

Diamond is the hardest rock. Some are not so hard.

diamond   granite   chalk   graphite   coal

Rocks are used to make many things. They are used to construct

The Taj Mahal is made of white marble. The Red Fort is made of red sandstone.

To the Teacher

It will be useful to tell the students to make rock collections and bring them to the class before you start the lesson. Bring some rocks yourself, which you feel children will not be able to find themselves. Show them the variety of rocks available by classifying them according to colour, according to smoothness, according to hardness and according to their ability to leave a mark, etc.

Diamond is used in jewellery.
It is also used for cutting glass.

Coal is used for burning.

Graphite is used to make the
'lead' of your pencil.

Talc, a very soft rock, is used
to make talcum powder.

Slate is used to make blackboards and
writing slates. It is also used to make
roofs of houses.

slate roof

Large rocks break to form smaller pieces. When these break further,
they form soil. Plants grow in this soil.

─LINKED INTERNET SITES─

The mystery of the floating rock
http://www.childrensmuseum.org/geomysteries/floatingrock/a1.html

Remember

1. Rock are of various shapes, sizes and colours.
2. Rocks are useful to us in many ways.
3. Soil is formed by breaking of rocks.

Exercises

1. Name these

(a) The hardest rock. ....

(b) A rock that can be used for writing. ....

(c) A rock that is not very hard. ....

(d) The Taj Mahal is made out of this rock. ....

(e) This rock is used in jewellery. ....

(f) A black rock used for burning. ....

2. Give the uses of these rocks. In some cases you may be able to find uses not given in this book. Mention them also.

(a) Talc ....

(b) Marble ....

(c) Slate ....

(d) Coal ....

3. How is soil formed? ....

....

Project

Make a rock collection

Pick up small pieces of rocks from various places. Pick them up from the garden, the playing field, from the roadside, from a place where a houses is being constructed, from the riverside or seaside and from any other place you visit. Some of these rocks have names. See how many you can name. Take the help of your teacher.

Revision Test Paper-5

1. Fill in the blanks.

(a) .... are hard and shiny.

(b) Glass is made from........................... .

(c) Houses made of snow are called ....

(d) .... is a very soft rock used to make talcum powder.

(e) The 'lead' in your pencils is made out of ....

2. Match the following:

(a) Iron   (i) Obtained from animals

(b) Wool and silk   (ii) Soil

(c) Heavy rain or snow   (iii) Marble

(d) Taj Mahal   (iv) Metal

(e) Breaking rocks   (v) Sloping roofs

3. From where do we get metals? ....

....

4. Name two materials each we get from

(a) Plants ....

(b) Animals ....

5. (a) Which is the hardest rock? ....

(b) Give two use of this rock. ....

....

6. (a) Name a material which can be made hard or soft.

....

(b) Name two things in your house made of this material.

....

7. In your note book draw a diagram of the tree which gives us cotton fibre.

20. Bones and Muscles

Warming Up!

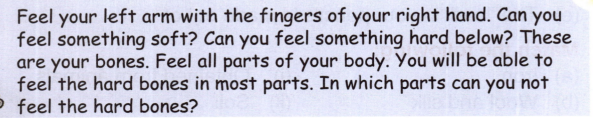

Feel your left arm with the fingers of your right hand. Can you feel something soft? Can you feel something hard below? These are your bones. Feel all parts of your body. You will be able to feel the hard bones in most parts. In which parts can you not feel the hard bones?

The top covering on your arm and most parts of your body is the **skin**. You can see hair growing on the skin at most places.

The soft parts below the skin are the **muscles**.
The hard parts are the **bones**.

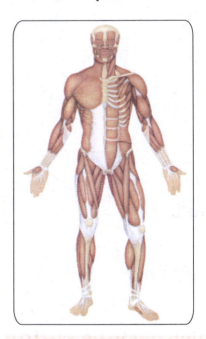

The hard bones support your body. If your hand did not have bones to support it, it would hang loose! You would not be able to use it.

Your bones together form the **skeleton**.

The skeleton gives your body its shape.

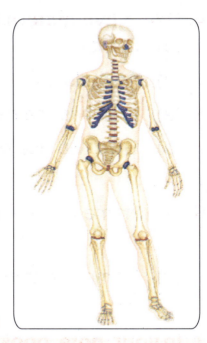

the body muscles   the skeleton

To the Teacher

Children may be inquisitive about and may have difficulty in understanding how joints help in movement. Show them how a door moves on its hinges and explain that the joints of the fingers, for example, move in a similar way. Help them in feeling their major muscles all over their body, and let them see how their thickness changes when body parts are moved.

• Movement

There are 206 bones in our skelton.
They are joined together.
At many of these joints the bones can move
over one another.
That is why you can move your hands, your
fingers, your legs and other parts of your body.

Feel the joints in your fingers. Move your fingers
and feel how the bones move.
Feel the joints at the elbow, shoulder and knee.
Can you feel joints at other places too?

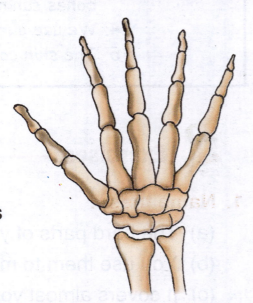

your hand is made up of
a number of bones joined together

Your bones cannot move on their own. Muscles make them move.
Muscles are attached to the bones. Feel the muscles in the front of your
arm, above the elbow. These are powerful muscles called **biceps**. When
you want to lift a book, the biceps pull at the bones in your hand.

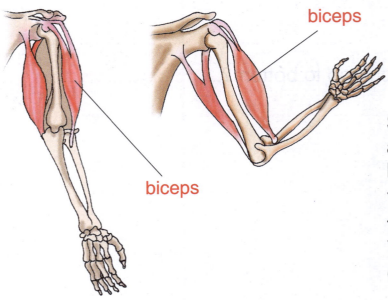

biceps

biceps

Similarly your leg muscles pull
at the bones in your legs and
help you to walk, jump and run.

You need strong muscles to run
fast or to be good at games.
You need proper food and
exercise to make your muscles.

Exercises

1. Name these:

(a) The hard parts of your body. ....

(b) You use them to move the bones. ....

(c) It covers almost your entire body. ....

(d) It gives you body its shape. ....

2. How can you make your muscles strong? ....

....

3. What do you think would happen if

(a) you had no bones? ....

....

(b) you had only one bone from top to bottom? ....

....

Measure biceps

Ask a friend to extend his or her arms.
Measure the thickness around the upper arm.
Now ask him or her to bend the arm.
Measure the thickness of the arm again.
Do you see any difference?
The biceps become shorter and harder to move
the arm. Do the same with your other friends.
Fill in table.

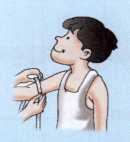

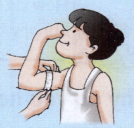

Name	Thickness of extended arm	Thickness of bent arm	Difference

21. Food

How do you feel if you do not eat for a long time? Besides feeling hungry do you feel weak? Why do you think we need food?

• Why do you need food?

You cannot live without food.

- Food gives you **energy** to work and play.
- Food enables your body to **grow**.
- Food helps your body **fight against diseases**.

To be healthy you need many different foods. Food can be divided into four groups. You need food from these four groups every day.

• Types of food

1. These foods help you to grow. They build your bones and muscles.

To the Teacher

We introduce here the main nutrients in food - proteins, sugars and starches, fats, vitamins and minerals - and their functions, without, of course, naming them. Do get children to examine their own diets and suggest changes if they find them defective. Parents, who complain that children do not drink milk of eat dal, will thank you for this!

2. Some foods give you energy to work and play. These foods give you quick energy.

sugar

3. These foods also give you energy which your body can store. It can be used later when needed.

4. These foods help your body to fight against diseases.

vegetables

fruits

Beside these foods, your body needs plenty of water every day.
If you do not drink enough water, especially on hot days, you can fall ill.

Most things you drink have water in them.

Most people need 4 - 6 glasses of water every day. You may need more during summer months.

soup

milk

some foods with plenty of water

• Good eating habits

1. You should eat at proper meal times. Avoid eating between meals. Write down your meal times.

Breakfast: _____   Lunch: _____   Dinner: _____

2. Eat clean food.

Dirty food and water have germs in them. They can make you ill.

do not eat dirty food

3. Wash your hands with soap and water before eating.

Utensils in which you eat should also be clean.

4. Stale food may have germs in it. You should either eat fresh food, or food that has been properly stored.

Some foods such as milk, meat, fruits and vegetables go bad very quickly. They should be stored in a refrigerator.

5. Always chew your food well. Never eat your food in a hurry.

LINKED INTERNET SITES

To learn about some ways to keep yourself healthy:
http://www.coolfoodplanet.org/gb/home.htm

Remember

1. Some foods help you to grow.
2. Some foods give you energy to work and play.
3. Some foods give you energy to store.
4. Some foods help your body to fight diseases.
5. To be healthy you need food from all these four groups. You also need plenty of water.
6. You should have good eating habits.

Exercises

1. Name two food items from each of these groups.

(a) Foods that give you quick energy. ....

(b) Foods that give energy to store. ....

(c) Foods that help you to grow. ....

(d) Foods that help fight diseases. ....

2. Make some good eating rules that everyone should follow.

(a) Eat food from all the four .... every day.

(b) Drink plenty of .... every day.

(c) Eat at proper ....

(d) Do not eat or drink .... food or water.

(e) Eat .... food or food that has been properly stored.

(f) Always .... your food properly.

3. Why should you not eat dirty or stale food? ....

....

Project

Do you eat the right food?

1. List what you ate yesterday and complete the table.

What I ate	Food group	What I ate	Food group
Breakfast		*Snacks*	
Bread			
Lunch		*Dinner*	

Now, count how many things you ate from each group.

22. Be Safe

Warming Up!

Have you ever hurt yourself? How?

Have you hurt yourself while playing with matchsticks or fireworks?

Have you hurt yourself while using a knife or scissors?

Have you hurt yourself while crossing the road, or while getting down from a moving bus?

Some things are dangerous. You have to be careful, otherwise you will hurt yourself.

• On the road

Remember that roads are not meant for playing. Playing on the roads can be dangerous.

Always walk on the footpath. Use the **zebra crossing** to cross the road.

Before crossing the road, look to your right, then to your left, and then to your right again. Now cross the road only if it is clear.

Remember, the green traffic light tells you to go. The red light tells you to stop.

To the Teacher

Listen to children's own experiences of getting hurt. Most safety rules will themselves come out of what they relate. This will make your job easier and also work better in convincing them to follow these rules.

At this stage you cannot keep the children away from some potentially dangerous things such as scissors or knives. They have to be instructed on how to use them properly.

Never lean out of a moving bus or car. You should also not try to get down from a moving bus.
Standing in a queue to board a bus is a good habit. It helps everyone.

• At home

Do not play with fire and electricity. They are very dangerous if not used properly. Use a matchstick only in the presence of an adult. Blow the matchstick out before throwing it in a dustbin.

Knives, scissors and tools are very useful to us. But we can get hurt if we are not careful with them. Ask your elders how to use them properly. Always use them in their presence.

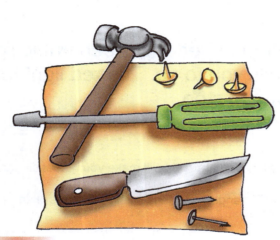

• At play

Follow the rules while playing a game. Do not try to hurt any player.

Always go to swim with elders. Do not go or jump into the deep end of the pool unless you are a good swimmer.

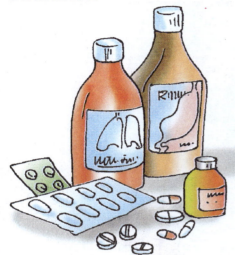

• Other safety rules

Never try to taste any medicines.

Never eat anything growing on plants that you do not know about.

These can be poisonous.

Never tease animals. They can bite or hurt you.

Loud sounds are bad for your ears. Never shout in anyone's ear.

Stand away from loud firecrackers and shut your ears when they go off.

Remember

1. Always follow safety rules on the road, at home or while playing.
2. Be very careful of fire, electricity and sharp things.

Exercises

1. Write whether dangerous or safe.

....

2. Name these:

(a) Traffic light that tells you to go. ....

(b) The place you should cross roads from. ....

(c) It can give you a dangerous shock. ....

(d) Bad for your ears. ....

(e) Always blow it out before throwing it away. ....

Are people safety conscious?

For one week carefully observe all the activities that your friends or other people do every day. Make a list of all dangerous things being done, in your exercise book.

For example your friend may be teasing a dog. Or a man may be teaching his child how to drive a car.

Tell the people why they should not do these things. How many people agreed with you? How many did not?

Do you think people in your neighborhood are safety conscious?

SAFETY CHART

Name of person	Dangerous activity	Did he agree or not

How many people agreed?......................They are safety conscious.

How many did not agree?......................They are not very safety conscious.

23. Our Environment

This is Mini's house.

This is Tinu's house.

List some things around Mini.

_____
_____
_____
_____
_____

These things make up the **environment** around Mini.

List some things around Tinu.

_____
_____
_____
_____
_____

These things make up the **environment** around Tinu.

• Activity

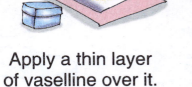

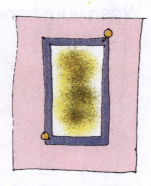

| Cut a strip of white cardboard. | Apply a thin layer of vaselline over it. | Hang it up in your classroom. | Observe it after 2 or 3 days. |

Can you see dirt sticking to the cardboard? _____

Where did the dirt come from?

(To the teacher : Initiate a class discussion. Let children come up with their own ideas. Then guide them to the right answer).

_____

_____

What things in your environment dirty the air?

_____

_____

What cleans the air?

_____

The air in a city has become dirty. It has become difficult to breathe.

What will you tell the people of the city to do, to clean the air?

(Class discussion. The teacher should discuss each suggestion (no matter how improbable it seems), and explain which ones are workable)

_____

_____

_____

• Activity

Wash your hands with soap and water and collect the water in a large bowl.

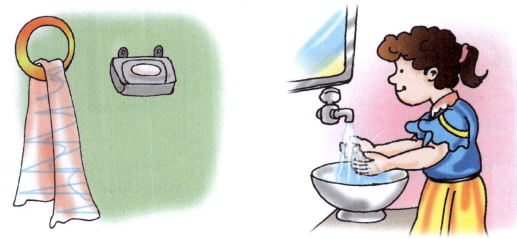

Observe the water. Has it become dirty?
Where did the dirt come from?
When you use soap and water to clean your body, the water becomes dirty.
When you flush your toilet, water takes away the dirt.
Where do you think all this dirty water goes?
(Class discussion)

It may go to a river or a lake in your city.

It may even go to the sea if your city is on the seashore. Dirty water from other houses in your city also goes there.

The water in the river, lake or sea becomes dirty.

A lot of dirty water also comes out of factories. it also dirties the river, lake or sea water.

Dirty water harms the fish, and plants growing in the water.

The water in your house may come from the same lake or river. It has to be cleaned before supplying to your house.

98

If it is not properly cleaned, you will fall sick if you drink the water.

You are lucky to have clean drinking water in your house. Lots of people in India do not have clean water to drink. Clean water is precious. You should never waste it.

Here are a few things you can do to save water.

- Never leave the tap running when you are not using the water.
- Do not let the tap run while brushing your teeth.
- If any tap is leaking, tell your parents, and ask them to have it repaired.
- When buying a new flush tank, ask your parents to buy one that uses less water.
- Be careful when watering the plants. Give the right amount of water.
- Do not give excess water, otherwise it will flow out and get wasted.
- If you find people wasting water, explain to them why the should not do so.

Exercises

1. We should plant more .... as they clean the air.

2. Smoke dirties the ....

3. Waste from houses and factories thrown into rivers dirties the ......

4. Drinking dirty water will make you ....

5. .... water is precious. We should not waste it.

Revision Test Paper-6

1. Fill in the blanks.

(a) The hard parts of your body are the ....

(b) A food that gives you quick energy is ....

(c) .... and .... help your body to fight against diseases.

(d) Stale food may have .... in it.

(e) You should use the .... crossing to cross a road.

2. Match the following:

(a) Body covering   (i) Skeleton

(b) Butter   (ii) Skin

(c) Bad for your ears   (iii) Strong muscles

(d) Gives shape to your body   (iv) Loud sounds

(e) Exercise and proper food   (v) Energy to store

3. Name two vegetarian and two non-vegetarian foods that children must eat, to grow.

Vegetarian ....

Non-vegetarian ....

4. Why are clean eating habits necessary? ....

....

5. How can you make your muscles strong? ....

....

6. Give one example each from the four groups of food. How does each group help you?

         Example   How it helps you

(a) ....

(b) ....

(c) ....

(d) ....